Animals Do What?

Animals Underwater

By Brenda McHale

Enslow Publishing

Published in 2023 by Enslow Publishing, LLC
29 East 21st Street, New York, NY 10010

This edition is published by arrangement with
Booklife Publishing

Edited by:
Emilie Dufresne

Designed by:
Dan Scase

Manufactured in the United States of America

CPSIA compliance information: Batch #CSENS23: For further information contact Enslow Publishing LLC, New York, New York at 1-800-398-2504.

Please visit our website, www.enslowpublishing.com.
For a free color catalog of all our high-quality books, call toll free 1-800-398-2504 or fax 1-877-980-4454.

Find us on

Cataloging-in-Publication Data

Names: McHale, Brenda.
Title: Animals underwater / Brenda McHale.
Description: New York : Enslow Publishing, 2023. |
Series: Animals do what? | Includes glossary and index.
Identifiers: ISBN 9781978531420 (pbk.) | ISBN 9781978531444 (library bound) | ISBN 9781978531437 (6 pack) | ISBN 9781978531451 (ebook)
Subjects: LCSH: Marine animals--Juvenile literature. | Marine ecology--Juvenile literature.
Classification: LCC QL122.2 M343 2023 | DDC 591.77--dc23

PHOTO CREDITS

All images are courtesy of Shutterstock.com. With thanks to Getty Images, Thinkstock Photo and iStockphoto. Front page – saulty72, Damsea. 1 – saulty72. 4&5 – Neel Adsul, wildestanimal, Ernie Hounshell, Jiang Zhongyan, Dan Kosmayer. 6&7 – frantisekhojdysz, Andaman. 8&9 – Steven L. Gordon, Vojce. 10&11 – Ewa Studio, photobeps, James Webb, Adam Ke. 12&13 – Tory Kallman, Neirfy, chonlasub woravichan. 14&15 – Vladimir Wrangel, Yellow Cat, ND700. 16&17 – Sophon K, Eric Isselee, Vladimir Wrangel, Malgorzata Litkowska. 18&19 – Gerald Robert Fischer, Kristina Vackova. 20&21 – Chase Dekker, Andrew Sutton. 22&23 – wildestanimal. Background on all pages – Damsea.

CONTENTS

Words that look like this can be found in the glossary on page 24.

WHAT LIVES UNDERWATER?

Some of the weirdest creatures on our planet live underwater. Here are some of the types of animals you can find there...

Fish such as sharks

Mammals such as walruses

Invertebrates such as squid

On each page you will see a fact file like this. It will give you cool facts about the animal, such as what type of animal it is, its diet, and where it lives.

SQUID

Type: Invertebrate (mollusk)

Found: Worldwide

Diet: Fish and crustaceans

WOBBEGONG

WOBBEGONG

Type: Vertebrate (fish)

Found: Pacific Ocean and Indian Ocean

Diet: Fish, octopuses, and crustaceans

The wobbegong is a type of shark. It is sometimes called the carpet shark.

The wobbegong lies on the seafloor like a shaggy rug. It sneaks up on creatures that come near it.

The tasselled wobbegong has tassels on its face that look like a beard.

A wobbegong's tassels and spotted pattern help it to be <u>camouflaged</u> at the bottom of the ocean.

It can very quickly open its mouth wide to suck in fish and crustaceans as they swim past.

SEAHORSE

NAME NOM *Animals Underwater* NO

SEAHORSE

Type: Vertebrate (fish)

Found: Warm and temperate waters

Diet: Small crustaceans

Seahorses sometimes like to swim in pairs with their tails linked, as though they are holding hands.

They're always eating because they have no teeth and no stomach, so food passes through them quickly.

Unlike many animals, it is the male seahorse that carries the eggs.

A male seahorse can give birth to over 1,000 babies at a time. Not many babies survive and sometimes a male seahorse might eat its own babies.

STARFISH

STARFISH

Type: Invertebrate
Found: Oceans worldwide
Diet: Clams, oysters, coral, and sponges

Starfish have an eye at the end of each arm. Each eye doesn't see very much, but starfish can see all around them.

Most starfish have five arms, but some can have as many as 15!

To eat, a starfish pushes its stomach outside its mouth to start breaking down parts of its prey.

It makes a food soup that it can slurp up.

Starfish have no brain, no blood, and no heart.

DOLPHIN

Animals Underwater

DOLPHIN

Type: Vertebrate (mammal)

Found: Oceans worldwide

Diet: Fish, octopuses, and other mammals

Dolphins "talk" to each other with clicks and whistles.

Dolphins have names. These are special sounds that are only used when "talking" to that dolphin.

To make friends, dolphins will stroke each other with their fins.

Dolphins need to come to the surface of the water to breathe.

They breathe through the blowhole on top of their heads.

When they sleep, half their brain stays awake and they keep one eye open. This means they can always watch for danger.

OCTOPUS

OCTOPUS

Type: Invertebrate (mollusk)

Found: Worldwide

Diet: Mollusks and crustaceans

Octopuses can change color. This helps them hide or warn other octopuses of danger.

Octopuses shoot water out backward to push them forward. A jet engine does the same with air.

Some types of octopus get up on two arms and run.

Giant Pacific octopuses are very smart. They can solve puzzles, open jars, and even copy other octopuses.

Octopuses have three hearts and blue blood!

If an octopus is in danger, it can spray ink at a predator. This helps it get away.

The suckers on an octopus's tentacles give the octopus a strong grip.

JELLYFISH

JELLYFISH

Type: Invertebrate

Found: Oceans worldwide

Diet: Ocean plants, crustaceans, and small sea creatures

Jellyfish eat and poop through the same hole.

Jellyfish do not have a heart, brain, or even eyes!

Many jellyfish don't swim. They are moved around by the ocean.

Jellyfish disappear when they are washed up on the beach. They are mostly made of water and will eventually <u>evaporate</u> in the air.

If you cut some jellyfish in half, the pieces will grow into two new jellyfish!

WARNING

DON'T TOUCH A JELLYFISH ON THE BEACH. IT MIGHT BE ONE THAT STINGS.

Box jellyfish are deadly. One jellyfish could kill up to 60 people.

PISTOL SHRIMP

The pistol shrimp uses its one large claw to shoot a very fast and very hot bubble at its prey.

PISTOL SHRIMP

Type: Invertebrate (crustacean)

Found: Coral reefs in warm ocean waters

Diet: Other crustaceans

This bubble can travel as fast as a car and is loud enough to break glass!

PEACOCK MANTIS SHRIMP

PEACOCK MANTIS SHRIMP

Type: Invertebrate (crustacean)

Found: Warm waters in the Indian Ocean and Pacific Ocean

Diet: Crabs and mollusks

The peacock mantis shrimp has one of the fastest punches in the world for its size.

Its punch is as fast as a bullet. This lets the shrimp punch through the shells of its prey.

BLUE WHALE

BLUE WHALE

Type: Vertebrate (mammal)

Found: Oceans worldwide

Diet: Tiny ocean animals

The blue whale is the world's largest living creature. It is bigger than anything that has ever lived — even dinosaurs!

A blue whale can be bigger than a boat.

A blue whale's heartbeat can be heard over 1.8 miles (3 km) away. That's because the heart is huge and weighs more than a cow.

They slow their heartbeat from around 35 beats per minute on the ocean's surface to two beats per minute when they're underwater.

Like other whales, blue whales breathe through blowholes.

NARWHAL

A narwhal's horn is really a tooth. It grows upward through its lip.

NARWHAL

Type: Vertebrate (mammal)

Found: Arctic waters

Diet: Fish and shellfish

The outside of the tusk is soft and sensitive. It's bendy at the end too.

All male narwhals grow a tusk, but only a few females do.

Sometimes two narwhals cross tusks and rub them together to clean them.

Narwhals can break through ice if they need to come to the surface to breathe.

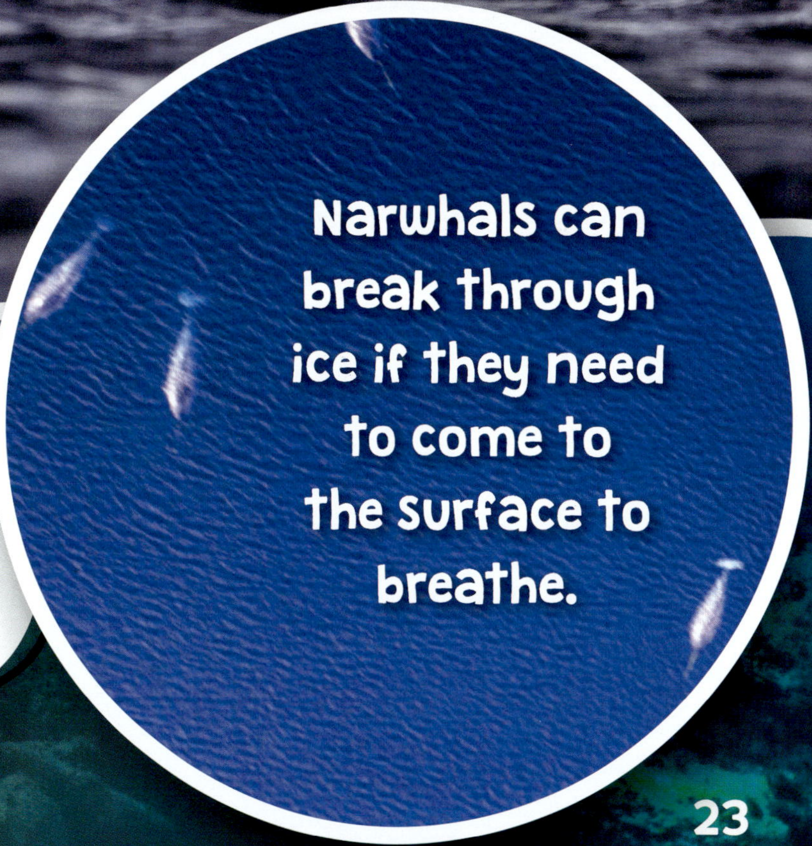

Narwhals gather in groups of hundreds or even thousands.

GLOSSARY

camouflaged	hidden by blending in with surroundings
crustaceans	animals that live in water and have a hard outer shell
diet	the kinds of foods that a person or animal usually eats
evaporate	to turn from a liquid into a gas or vapor, usually through heat
fish	an animal that lives in water, swims using fins, and breathes with gills
invertebrates	animals that do not have a backbone
mammals	animals that are warm-blooded, have a backbone, and produce milk to feed their young
mollusk	a creature with a soft body, no backbone, and usually a shell
predator	an animal that hunts other animals for food
prey	an animal that is eaten by another animal for food
temperate	a region or climate that has mild temperatures
vertebrate	an animal that has a backbone

INDEX